S0-BFC-048

TRAILBLAZERS of the MODERN WORLD

J. K. ROWLING

By Joan Price

WORLD ALMANAC® LIBRARY

Please visit our web site at: www.worldalmanaclibrary.com
For a free color catalog describing World Almanac® Library's list
of high-quality books and multimedia programs, call 1-800-848-2928 (USA)
or 1-800-387-3178 (Canada). World Almanac® Library's fax: (414) 332-3567.

Library of Congress Cataloging-in-Publication Data

Price, Joan.
    J. K. Rowling / by Joan Price.
       p. cm. — (Trailblazers of the modern world)
    Includes bibliographical references and index.
    ISBN 0-8368-5499-3 (lib. bdg.)
    ISBN 0-8368-5268-0 (softcover)
    1. Rowling, J. K.—Juvenile literature. 2. Authors, English—20th century—Biography—
Juvenile literature. 3. Potter, Harry (Fictitious character)—Juvenile literature. 4. Children's
stories—Authorship—Juvenile literature. I. Title. II. Series.
    PR6068.O93Z83   2004
    823'.914—dc22
    [B]   2004043400

First published in 2005 by
World Almanac® Library
330 West Olive Street, Suite 100
Milwaukee, WI 53212 USA

Copyright © 2005 by World Almanac® Library.

Project manager: Jonny Brown
Editor: Jim Mezzanotte
Design and page production: Scott M. Krall
Photo research: Diane Laska-Swanke
Indexer: Walter Kronenberg

Photo credits: © Alpha/Globe Photos: 4, 19, 40, 41; © Joe Alvarez/Alpha/Globe Photos: 29; © Chris Andrews; Chris Andrews Publications/CORBIS: 15; © AP/Wide World Photos: cover, 12, 31, 34, 36, 38; © Scott Barbour/Getty Images: 42; © Derek Croucher/CORBIS: 22; © Urbano Delvalle/Time Life Pictures/Getty Images: 33; © Amanda Edwards/Getty Images: 16; © Steve Finn/Alpha/Globe Photos: 23; © Globe Photos: 14; © Neil Jacobs/Getty Images: 39; © Noel Laura/CORBIS SYGMA: 26; © Kevin Lee/Getty Images: 7; © Murdo Macleod/CORBIS SYGMA: 27; © Ludovic Maisant/CORBIS: 20; © Ian Nicholson/AFP/Getty Images: 24; © Hugo Philpott/AFP/Getty Images: 5; Photofest: 6, 8, 9, 18, 25, 28, 35 bottom, 37; © Andrea Renault/Globe Photos: 13; © Nicholas Roberts/AFP/Getty Images: 35 top; © Chung Sung-Jun/Getty Images: 30; © Adam Woolfitt/CORBIS: 10

Printed in the United States of America

1 2 3 4 5 6 7 8 9 08 07 06 05 04

TABLE of CONTENTS

Words that appear in the glossary are printed in **boldface**
type the first time they occur in the text.

CHAPTER 1

RAGS TO RICHES

How did Joanne Rowling—a poor, single mother who could not afford a used typewriter, let alone a computer—become J. K. Rowling, best-selling author of the incredibly popular Harry Potter books? You don't need to be a wizard to find the answer. Rowling might have been poor, but she possessed an important treasure—her own imagination. By using that imagination, working hard, and never giving up despite many obstacles, Rowling created the story of Harry Potter, a young boy whose magical adventures have delighted millions of readers around the world.

J. K. Rowling has said, "I am an extraordinarily lucky person, doing what I love best in the world."

HARD TIMES

Joanne, or "Jo," Rowling has achieved fame and fortune with her Harry Potter books, but her life has not always been easy. In 1994, she separated from her husband and moved to Edinburgh, Scotland, where she lived in a dark, dingy apartment with her infant daughter. She had no job and little money. What she did have, however, was a suitcase full of notes about a special boy named Harry Potter and a strong desire to write a book. Living on **welfare** and struggling to make ends meet, she wrote whenever she could. In 1995, a year after moving to Edinburgh, she managed to complete *Harry Potter and the Philosopher's Stone.*

Although Rowling had finished her book, she was filled with doubt. Would anyone want to publish her book? Fearful but determined, she sent the **manuscript** to a **literary agent**. Even with the literary agent's help, she received many rejections, which only helped to confirm her doubts. Finally, however, the agent found a publisher that was willing to take a chance on the story of Harry Potter.

AN IDEA ON A TRAIN

Rowling has said that the idea for Harry Potter "fell into her head" while she was on a train in England going from Manchester to London, where she lived at the time. As soon as she got off the train, Rowling hurried home to her apartment to begin writing her story about an English orphan who has a miserable life with his aunt and uncle and their dreadful son, Dudley. But all that changes when a mysterious letter arrives by owl messenger telling Harry that he is the son of wizards. Harry goes off to the Hogwarts School of Wizardry and his magical adventures begin.

Children and adults wave goodbye to J. K. Rowling as she departs London's Cross station in an old steam train on July 8, 2000. She is traveling to the north of England to promote her latest Harry Potter book.

A STRANGE BUT FAMILIAR WORLD

Jo Rowling has always liked to dream of faraway lands, of wizards and strange animals. "When you dream, you can do what you like," she has said. In her Harry Potter books, however, she mixes fantasy with everyday life

Harry Potter (right) flies on his broomstick in the movie *Harry Potter and the Chamber of Secrets.*

and writes about universal themes—such as the struggle between good and evil—that are familiar to most people.

In the unique world of Harry Potter, there are good wizards such as Professor Dumbledore and bad wizards such as the evil Lord Voldemort. There are ghosts, who—like people we meet in real life—can be friendly or nasty. Mail gets delivered, just as it does in the real world, but it is delivered by owls. The Hogwarts campus resembles an ordinary English boarding school, but it is inhabited by strange creatures such as hippogriffs and pet rats. Students chase after balls—but on broomsticks! Beyond school grounds, unicorns and gigantic spiders walk through the Forbidden Forest. The students enjoy eating candy, but they eat Chocolate Frogs and Every Flavor Beans, with flavors that include spinach, earwax, and vomit. Like all children, they sometimes make mistakes and sometimes behave badly, and they may find themselves in situations where they will have to overcome their fears.

A Dream Come True

Rowling had not expected her books to be so wildly successful. In an interview, she said, "I would have been crazy to have expected what has happened to Harry. The mere fact of being able to say I was a published author was the fulfillment of a dream I've had since I was a very young child."

WILD ABOUT HARRY

For Jo Rowling, the success of Harry Potter has been a fantasy all its own. The book *Harry Potter and the Philosopher's Stone* (entitled *Harry Potter and the Sorcerer's Stone* in the

United States) was a hit with both children and adults. It sold so well that Rowling's British and U.S. publishers had to print hundreds of thousands of extra copies. The success of the book became news on television and in newspapers and magazines, and the book won the British Book Awards' Children's Book of the Year in 1997.

Harry Potter, it turned out, had only just begun. Rowling intended to publish a total of seven books about Harry Potter—one for every year Harry would be at wizard school—and she kept writing. Readers, meanwhile, became hooked on the books' memorable characters, humor, and intriguing plots, and they kept buying. By the summer of 2003, the first five Harry Potter books were among the most popular in the world. In fact, *Harry Potter and the Goblet of Fire*, the fourth book in the series, became a best-seller weeks before it was even released! (People had ordered it before its release.) The Harry Potter books continue to be in or near the top of the best-seller lists, and movies based on the books have been a huge smash at the box office.

The success of Harry Potter is about more than just selling a lot of books. In a way, J. K. Rowling—the single mother who dared to realize her dreams—actually started a small revolution. Today, in an age when many children often spend their free time watching television or playing video games, Jo Rowling's Harry Potter books have introduced many young people to the wonders of reading. Using their own imaginations, they discover the best magic of all—turning the page to find out what happens next!

Two young fans stand in front of a poster for a Harry Potter movie in Beijing, China, in 2002.

CHAPTER 2

GROWING UP

Jo Rowling's parents, Anne Volant and Pete Rowling, met on a train while traveling to Arbroath, Scotland, in 1963. They fell in love and soon married. The newlyweds moved into a small home in Chipping Sodbury, England, which is near the city of Bristol. Pete worked at the Bristol Rolls-Royce factory, which made airplane engines. Anne was a lab technician.

Professor Dumbledore and Harry Potter in Harry Potter and the Chamber of Secrets

Weird Names

Many interesting names can be found in the Harry Potter books—"Dumbledore," for example, and "Voldemort." Rowling made up some of these names, but she also used names she came across in real life. Rowling has said that the funny-sounding name of her birthplace probably "doomed" her to a love of collecting weird names.

EARLY CHILDHOOD

Joanne Rowling was born on July 31, 1965, at Chipping Sodbury General Hospital. Two years later, her sister Dianne, or "Di," was born at home. On that day, Pete gave Jo some Play-Doh to keep her busy. Jo Rowling does not recall the first time she saw her baby sister, but she does remember eating the Play-Doh!

Both Anne and Pete loved to read, and they often read to their children. According to Jo, her mother was "never happier than when she was curled up reading. That was a big influence on me."

When Jo was five, she began making up stories and telling them to Di. These stories were often about rabbits, because both Jo and Di "badly wanted a rabbit" for a pet. She made up a story about Di "falling down a rabbit hole and ... [being] fed strawberries by the rabbit family inside it."

At age six, Jo recalls, she wrote her first story about "a rabbit called Rabbit. He got the measles and was visited by his friends, including a giant bee called Miss Bee." From then on, Jo knew she wanted to be a writer. But she was too embarrassed to tell anyone about her ambition, and she kept it a secret.

In 1971, the Rowlings moved to Winterbourne, England. Jo and Di became close friends with their young neighbors, Ian and Vikki Potter. The four children would straddle broomsticks and race around the yard pretending to fly, and they often dressed up as witches and wizards. As a witch, Jo would pretend to make up witches' brews of yucky ingredients.

Harry Potter (center) is showered by letters as the Dursleys look on in panic in the movie *Harry Potter and the Sorcerer's Stone.*

Inspiration for a Name

As a child, Jo Rowling liked Ian and Vikki Potter's last name better than her own because other kids always teased her about her name, making jokes about rolling pins (her name sounds a lot like the word "rolling"). According to Rowling, the Potter family inspired Harry Potter's last name.

Chepstow Castle on the River Wye. When Jo Rowling and her sister Di were children, they used to explore around the castle and wander through the fields along the river.

In 1974, when Jo was nine, the Rowling family moved to Tutshill, a small village in a rural area of England called the Forest of Dean. The family lived in a cottage next to a church and a graveyard. Jo's friends thought it was spooky living next to a graveyard, but Jo liked it—the graveyard was a great source of names. Before the new school year began, Jo and Di spent their days wandering happily through fields and along the River Wye. Jo would imagine fantasy stories and adventures at Chepstow Castle, which sits high on a cliff overlooking the river. But these fun-filled days ended when she entered her new school.

Jo has said that her new teacher, Mrs. Morgan, "scared the life out of me." On the first day of school, Mrs. Morgan gave an arithmetic test to separate the "smart" students from the "stupid" ones. The test was on fractions. Jo had never done fractions before, so she failed. Mrs. Morgan sat Jo in a desk on her far right—

An Unkind Teacher

In her Harry Potter books, Jo Rowling based the character of Professor Snape, the cruel Potions Master at Hogwarts School, after Mrs. Morgan—the teacher who labeled students "smart" and "stupid" and initially put Jo in the "stupid" row because she had not yet learned fractions.

the "stupid" row. When Mrs. Morgan finally decided that Jo was "smart," she moved her to the left.

Although Jo hated school, she loved to read. One of her favorite books was *The Little White Horse*, by Elizabeth Goudge. She remembers that the main character "was a very interesting heroine—she wasn't beautiful, she was nosy, she had a temper. She was human, in a word, when a lot of girl characters tend not to be." Many years later, Jo Rowling would create similar characters for her Harry Potter books.

Above all, Jo loved to write. She wrote a short novel called *The Seven Cursed Diamonds*, but she tucked it away. She never showed her writing to anyone, except for her sister Di.

The "K" in "J. K."

Jo's grandparents, Ernie and Kathleen Rowling, ran a grocery store and lived in an apartment above the store. When Jo and Di came to visit, Ernie and Kathleen would let them go downstairs and play "store." Jo and Di always looked forward to these visits. They had a close relationship with their grandparents and it was a blow to nine-year-old Jo when Kathleen Rowling died. "I adored her," she said, "and my saddest memory of that time is of her death." Jo was born without a middle name, but she later honored her grandmother by using the middle initial "K" in her **pen name**— J. K. Rowling.

In 1976, Jo entered Wyedean Comprehensive Secondary School (roughly equivalent to middle school and high school combined in the United States). Although she made high grades, she often felt anxious and insecure. "I was quiet, freckly, short-sighted and rubbish at sports," she recalled. "I am the only person I know who managed to break their arm playing **netball**."

Jo's favorite subject was English. She also excelled in foreign languages and liked to sketch in pen and ink. In school, she often doodled on her notepad as well as on pages in her textbooks. She didn't mind showing her artwork to others, but she never showed her writing and never told anyone that she wanted to be a writer.

Jo Rowling holds a copy of her new book, *Harry Potter and the Order of the Phoenix*, in June 2003 at a bookstore in Edinburgh.

Jessica Mitford

At age fourteen, Jo read *Hons and Rebels* (entitled *Daughters and Rebels* in the United States), an autobiography by the British writer Jessica Mitford. Mitford was a **muckraker** and **feminist** who had fought in the Spanish Civil War in the 1930s when she was only nineteen. The book made a lasting impression on Jo Rowling. She admired Jessica Mitford's courage to follow her convictions, which often led her into dangerous situations. During the U.S. **civil rights** movement of the 1960s, for example, Mitford had once been barricaded in a Baptist church with the Rev. Martin Luther King Jr. as a white mob rioted outside. She advocated for poor people incapable of fighting for themselves. In writing *The American Way of Death*, a book that exposed the corruption of the American funeral business, Jessica and her husband helped make reasonably priced funeral expenses available for underprivileged families. She actively defended the right of all people to express their political and social views.

At book signings, Jo Rowling sometimes meets children who dress up to look like Harry Potter!

On a class trip to Stratford-on-Avon, Jo saw William Shakespeare's *The Winter's Tale*, a play in which the leading female character is named Queen Hermione. The name Hermione caught Jo's attention. Years later, she gave the name to Harry Potter's friend, Hermione Granger. Jo Rowling has said that Hermoine Granger's personality is very much like her own.

ILLNESS STRIKES

When Jo was fifteen, her mother Anne was diagnosed with multiple sclerosis, or "MS," a slow, weakening disease that affects the nervous system. There is no known cure for MS. A person suffering from MS may have no symptoms for periods of time, but the disease becomes progressively worse and may cause vision problems, hand tremors, slurred speech, and even paralysis of an arm or leg. Jo had to watch her mother's physical decline knowing she was helpless to fight against it.

Harry Potter and Ron Weasley narrowly avoid disaster as they fly the Ford Anglia in *Harry Potter and the Chamber of Secrets*.

A "Magic" Car

One of the bright spots in Jo's senior year of secondary school was a new friend, Sean Harris. Sean had a turquoise Ford Anglia, and for Jo it spelled freedom from a dull social life. Sean and Jo would drive everywhere, sharing with each other their plans to make a difference in the world. Rowling modeled the character Ron Weasley after Sean, and she dedicated the second Harry Potter book to him. She also paid tribute to Sean's Ford Anglia by making it the magic flying car that rescues Harry from his aunt, uncle, and cousin the summer before his second year at Hogwarts, "just as the car rescued me from my boredom."

COLLEGE AND BEYOND

During the summer of 1983, Jo enrolled at the University of Exeter. She wanted to study English so she could become a better writer, but her parents urged her to major in French. They insisted that knowing a foreign language would improve her chances of landing a good secretary job. Jo hated the idea of being a secretary—all she really wanted was to be a writer. She did not have the courage to tell anyone about her dream, however, and she took her parents' advice.

LIFE IN COLLEGE

Jo had imagined that she would become an **activist** in college—just like one of her favorite writers, Jessica Mitford, who fought for civil rights, racial equality, and other causes. But college wasn't the place of radical protest she had expected. The University of Exeter, Rowling recalled to a reporter, "was fantastic, but it did not offer quite the chance to be a radical that I planned."

A shy young woman, Jo spent a lot of time alone writing, sketching, and playing her guitar. She also collected odd names from **mythology** and literature— "names from saints, place-names, war memorials, gravestones." Finally, she made friends with some like-minded students and met her first boyfriend. She lined her eyes with mascara, got contact lenses so she didn't have to

Oxford University, England. Some scenes featuring Hogwarts School in the Harry Potter movies were filmed at this university.

wear glasses, spent time with her friends at the Black Horse pub in town, and in general started having fun.

Jo spent her third year of college in Paris, where she was a teaching assistant in English. She particularly loved that year. When she returned to England, however, her mother could no longer walk. Anne Rowling attended Jo's college graduation in a wheelchair with her husband Pete by her side.

A poster for an Amnesty International campaign to end violence against women.

FINDING WORK

Once Jo had graduated, she needed to get a job. Writing was her love, but she had to eat, and writing stories that she did not send to publishers wasn't going to pay the rent. To improve her job opportunities, she enrolled in a **bilingual** secretary course. When Jo finished the course, she donned a suit for job interviews. Although she hated the interviews, they did lead to Jo finding part-time jobs filling in for full-time secretaries during their vacations. "Unfortunately," she said, "I am one of the most disorganized people in the world and, as I later proved, the worst secretary ever."

After a series of uninteresting secretarial jobs, Jo accepted a position with Amnesty International, an organization that seeks to prevent and end human rights abuses all over the world. Jo's job with the organization involved researching human rights abuses in French-speaking African countries. If she couldn't write full-time she wanted to stand up for human rights like her hero, Jessica Mitford. During lunch hours, however, she would rush to a cafe or pub to write.

HARRY POTTER IS BORN

When Jo's college boyfriend found a job in the city of Manchester, he asked Jo to leave London and move to Manchester with him. She agreed and joined him in Manchester to look for an apartment. On the ride back from Manchester to London, the train suddenly ground to a halt. The conductor announced that a mechanical problem would delay the train at least four hours. With nothing to do but wait, she sat looking out the window at a herd of cows grazing in a meadow. All of a sudden, she later recalled, the character of Harry Potter came into her head. She imagined Harry as an orphan boy being raised by a cruel aunt and uncle. Harry has no idea that he is a wizard until he is whisked off to a boarding school for young wizards.

Jo Rowling had never been so excited by an idea in her life. She knew immediately that the book she had in mind would be fun to write. She wasn't thinking it would be a book for children—she just knew it would be about a special boy named Harry Potter.

On the train, Jo quickly searched for a pen, but she didn't have one that worked. Rather than writing her thoughts down, she had to commit them to memory. First she concentrated on the Hogwarts School of Witchcraft and Wizardry and some of the wizards and creatures that would inhabit it. As she thought out the plot, names of her characters popped into her

Harry Potter uses his magic wand to cast a spell in *Harry Potter and the Chamber of Secrets.*

A Child with Power

In an interview, Jo talked about her original vision of Harry Potter. "At that point," she said, "it was essentially the idea for a boy who didn't know he was a wizard, and the wizard school he ended up going to. ... The idea that we could have a child who escapes from the confines of the adult world and goes somewhere where he has power, both literally and metaphorically, really appealed to me."

mind—Ron, Hermione, Hagrid, and Dumbledore. Her excitement grew. When she returned to her London apartment that night, she wrote everything down.

After her move to Manchester, Jo found a temporary secretarial job, but she was soon laid off. She has said that all she ever liked about working as a secretary was being able to type her "Harry Potter story on the computer when no one was looking." She admits to "not taking very reliable minutes in meetings," because she was usually jotting notes about her book in the margins, drawing images, or dreaming up more names and characters. She decided there would be seven Harry Potter books, one for each of Harry's years at Hogwarts.

A TERRIBLE BLOW

Anne Rowling died on December 30, 1990, at age forty-five. Jo had seen her mother just before Christmas and later recalled that "she was extremely thin and looked exhausted." For a long time after her mother's death, Jo couldn't write about her without crying.

Harry Potter (center), Ron Weasley (right), and Hermione Granger walk down some steps at Hogwarts School of Witchcraft and Wizardry in the movie *Harry Potter and the Prisoner of Azkaban*.

In the first Harry Potter book, there is a chapter entitled "The Mirror of Erised." This magical mirror reflects the image a person most desires to see ("erised" is "desire" spelled backwards). In Harry's case, he sees his dead parents waving, with his mother smiling and crying at the same time. A reporter once asked Jo what she would say to her mother if she could speak to her in the Mirror of Erised for a few short minutes. Jo replied that, like any child, she would update her mother on everything that was happening in her life, and that she would not think to ask her mother, until it was too late, the most important question of all—"what it is really like to be dead."

The fantasy world of Harry Potter excited Jo Rowling, but for awhile she stuck with her boring secretarial jobs. Months after her mother's death, however, Jo realized that her relationship with her boyfriend was coming to an end. She needed to move on.

CHAPTER 4

NEW HORIZONS

Losing her mother shook Jo's already rocky world. Her relationship with her boyfriend was over and she had quit her job. To make matters worse, a thief broke into her apartment in Manchester shortly after her mother died. Among the items stolen were all of the sentimental objects that Anne Rowling had left to Jo. The only thing that got Jo through this "nightmare period" was writing about Harry Potter.

A FRESH START

Oporto, Portugal.
In Oporto, Jo Rowling met and married Jorge Arantes and gave birth to her daughter Jessica.

Jo knew that office work was not for her, but she still needed to work. She had enjoyed teaching in Paris, so she looked in the paper for a teaching job. A position that jumped out at her was one for English teachers in Oporto, Portugal. The idea of going to a new place both excited and frightened her, but she was determined to start a new life. She applied for the teaching job and was accepted.

The move to Portugal allowed Jo to make a fresh start. She left Manchester with just a few personal belongings and a box full of notes for the Harry Potter book. When Jo arrived in Oporto, she did not have to look for a place to live, because the school officials had found an

apartment for her to share with two other new teachers. At first Jo was homesick, but her new roommates—Aine Kiely, from Ireland, and Jill Prewett, from England— soon had her laughing, and they became special and lasting friends. In fact, Jo dedicated the third Harry Potter book, *Harry Potter and the Prisoner of Azkaban*, to these two friends. She called them the "godmothers of Swing," in reference to a disco called Swing that the three women often went to on weekends in Oporto.

Jo enjoyed her new life in Oporto. Her students liked her immediately, and, because she taught afternoons and evenings, she had her mornings free to write. She resumed her habit of writing in cafes, especially a place called the Café Majestic. Sometimes she cried as she wrote about Harry's life as an orphan, because she was reminded of the passing of her own mother.

MARRIAGE AND MOTHERHOOD

One night while Jo and her friends were in a disco, she met Jorge Arantes, a television journalist. She liked his dark, good looks and quick smile, and he found himself immediately attracted to her. As they began to date, both were happy to discover they shared a fondness for books. They fell in love, but almost from the start their relationship suffered from jealousy and arguments. Ignoring these warning signs, they married on October 16, 1992. Jo became pregnant soon after the wedding.

Jo and Jorge were elated about the pregnancy, and the first months of their marriage were good if somewhat hectic at times. Their work schedules often conflicted, and it was hard to find private time together. Still, Jo was happy in their marriage and Jorge inspired her writing. She continued to teach and to write.

As Jo's pregnancy progressed, however, her relationship with Jorge grew more strained and unstable. Jorge, always working, was often absent from their home, and he did not show Jo the kindness she needed. Jo fell into a deep depression.

On July 27, 1993, four days before her twenty-eighth birthday, Jo Rowling gave birth to a baby girl. She named the child Jessica, after her hero, Jessica Mitford. For Jo, the best thing to happen to her during her marriage and "without doubt the best moment of my life" was the birth of her daughter. But the new baby could not save her crumbling marriage to Jorge.

"I was very depressed," Jo told a reporter. "And having a newborn child made it doubly difficult. I simply felt like a non-person. I was very low and I felt I had to achieve something." At that point, she had completed only the first three chapters of *Harry Potter and the Philosopher's Stone*. The rest of the book was in rough draft. Under the circumstances, she could not put her mind to writing. Her teaching job was over for the summer holidays, and her marriage had fallen apart.

Edinburgh, Scotland. Jo Rowling moved from Portugal to Edinburgh to be close to her sister Di. Jo and her family continue to live in Edinburgh today.

MOVING TO EDINBURGH

In the midst of her despair, Jo received a telephone call from her sister Di, who had married and was attending law school in Edinburgh, Scotland. Di asked Jo to move to Edinburgh so they could be closer, and Jo agreed.

In Edinburgh, Jo knew only her sister and her sister's best friend. Most of Jo's friends lived in London, but she wanted to be near Di and thought that Edinburgh was a good city to bring up her child. Not wanting to burden her sister, but having very little money, Jo moved into an unheated apartment in a run-down part of the city. It was not a nice place to live—for Jo or her daughter. "I never expected to mess up so badly that I would find myself in an unheated mouse-infested **flat**, looking after my daughter," she later told a reporter. "And I was angry because I felt that I was letting her down."

IMPORTANT ENCOURAGEMENT

One dreary afternoon when Jo was visiting her sister, she began telling Di the story of Harry Potter, just as she had told her the story of Rabbit when they were children. Di was excited by the story and asked if she could read what Jo had written so far. Reluctantly, Jo gave her sister the first three chapters. Di loved the story. Jo has said that if Di hadn't liked the story, at a time when Jo was feeling so low about herself, she is not sure what Harry's future might have been.

By that time, she had already been working on the plots for the seven-book series for more than three years. But Di did like the story, and she gave Jo the encouragement to carry on.

Jo Rowling has never forgotten her struggles as a single parent. Today, she gives her time and money to the National Council for One Parent Families.

DARK DAYS

Although Jo was happy to be near her sister, she again fell into a deep depression. She had a baby to care for, she was in a strange place, and she had no job. Jo had planned to get a job to make ends meet while she wrote *Harry Potter and the Philosopher's Stone*, but she needed someone to watch Jessica while she worked. She could get some money for childcare from the British public assistance system—what is called "welfare" in the United States—but not if she had a job.

Jo Rowling speaks in London at the National Council for One Parent Families Conference.

Jo had good reason to feel reluctant about going on welfare. A month after she and Jessica arrived in Edinburgh, the British prime minister, John Major, made a speech sharply criticizing single parents for being welfare-loving freeloaders. He stated that women on public assistance were lazy and purposefully avoided work. Single mothers, he said, were to blame for the problems of young people in England. Jo felt deeply hurt by Major's speech, and she took it to heart. She might have been a single mother, but she was also a college graduate who wanted to find a teaching job.

In order to teach in Scotland, Jo would have to go back to school for some additional courses. She would need a year to complete these courses. How could she, a single mother, take the necessary course work when she had no money and a baby to support? Finally, she decided she would go on welfare while she was in school. She went through many interviews, and she had to explain how she came to be penniless and the sole caretaker of her child. At last, the government approved a small amount of money. But it was not nearly enough to cover her school costs, food, clothes, and rent.

One day, when Jo was visiting a friend of her sister, she happened to notice the number of toys the woman's son had. At that point, all of Jessica's toys could have fit into a shoebox. Jo went home and cried. Soon after, a **social worker** brought a few used toys for Jessica: a worn-out teddy bear, a little plastic house, and a beat-up plastic telephone. Jo was so ashamed that she stuffed the toys into a garbage bag and threw it away. During this dark time, she began seeing a **counselor** to help her sort through her feelings.

Welfare Mothers

Jo Rowling never forgot British prime minister John Major's speech in which he criticized single mothers on welfare for being freeloaders. In an interview, she said, "I had no intention, no desire, to remain on benefits. It's the most soul-destroying thing. I don't want to dramatize, but there were nights when, though Jessica ate, I didn't. The suggestion that you would deliberately make yourself entitled ... You'd have to be a complete idiot."

Madame Hooch watches with astonishment as Neville Longbottom takes to the air on a broomstick in *Harry Potter and the Sorcerer's Stone.*

CHAPTER 5

A TURNING POINT

Children in the United States celebrate the publication of *Harry Potter and the Goblet of Fire.*

In the summer of 1994, Jo filed for divorce from Jorge, who still lived in Portugal. She also made a big decision. Completing the courses she needed in order to teach would take a year. She knew that unless she made a push to finish the first Harry Potter book right away, she might never finish it. So Jo Rowling made herself a promise. She would finish the Harry Potter book in a year and try to get it published. Jo realized she was setting herself up for a difficult time, but she also knew she had to try. She thought, "What is the worst that could happen? Every publishing company in Britain could turn me down. Big deal."

Jo wrote furiously. When she wasn't writing, taking graduate courses, or going to counseling, she was tending to Jessica and looking for part-time work. Her tiny apartment was unfurnished, so friends lent her pieces of furniture and some household items. She could not afford a computer or even a used typewriter, so she wrote the adventures of Harry Potter on pieces of scrap paper.

Although Jo found a part-time secretarial job, she could not go off welfare, because the job did not pay enough to support her and Jessica. If Jo did take a full-time job, she would lose the welfare benefits and have no time to write. Begrudgingly, she stuck with the part-time job, stayed on welfare, and kept writing.

A PLACE TO WRITE

Jo could not face doing all of her writing in her cold, dark apartment. She went looking for cafes, where she had always loved to write. On her budget, however, she could not afford to spend afternoons drinking cups of expensive coffee, and most cafes did not want her to use a table for hours without spending money.

During this difficult time, Di's husband Roger became part owner of Nicolson's Café, which was not far from Jo's apartment. Roger welcomed her to come in to write. Nicolson's, Jo soon discovered, was a perfect place for writing. No one in the cafe minded if she ordered one cup of coffee and nursed it for a few hours, writing with Jessica in a stroller by her side.

The staff at Nicolson's liked Jo. They often warmed up her coffee but gave her the privacy she needed. She used to joke about what she would do for them if she ever got published and the book sold well.

Jo Rowling works on a Harry Potter manuscript in an Edinburgh coffee shop.

Nicolson's Café

Once Jo Rowling had a place to write, she fell into a routine. Every day, Jo would put Jessica in a stroller and walk her around town. When Jessica fell asleep, Jo would walk over to Nicolson's. The cafe had a pleasant decor, with blue and yellow tablecloths and prints of paintings by Henri Matisse on the walls. Jo would slide behind her favorite table in the corner, buy a cup of coffee, and position the stroller so she could keep an eye on her daughter. While Jessica slept, Jo took out her notebook and wrote. She wrote everything in longhand. When Jessica woke up, usually in two or three hours, Jo put away her writing and left the cafe.

She still wasn't sure, however, that she would ever be published. Looking back, she said, "It's true that I wrote in Nicolson's café with my daughter sleeping beside me. That sounds very romantic but of course it's not at all romantic when you are living through it."

Harry Potter (left) and his best friend Ron Weasley attend class at Hogwarts School for Witchcraft and Wizardry in *Harry Potter and the Chamber of Secrets*.

KEEPING A PROMISE

Jo hated the end of each week, when she had to go to the post office to cash her welfare check. To this day, she has not forgotten the shame she felt when she handed her welfare check over the counter, in front of people who might have held the same opinion as Prime Minister Major. It was one of the lowest points in her life. "My self-respect was on the floor."

Writing *Harry Potter and the Philosopher's Stone* saw her through the tough times. She was writing well and her imagination soared. The pages piled up. She wasn't trying to write a best-selling children's book. She wrote Harry Potter for herself, creating a fantasy world that she enjoyed.

But as Jo got closer to completing the book, some of her old fears came flooding back. She would have to send the manuscript to a publisher, and what if no one liked it? Nevertheless, she had promised herself that she would complete the book in a year and send it out. No matter what the risk of rejection, she would keep that promise.

A FINISHED MANUSCRIPT

The year 1995 became a turning point in Jo's life. Through the generosity of a friend, she went off welfare in the summer. Now Jo could afford to send Jessica to daycare while she finished her coursework full-time. On weekends, she would sneak into the college computer laboratory to type her manuscript. Jessica sat at her feet "working her way through piles of jigsaws." Jo lived in constant fear that someone would discover she was typing her manuscript rather than doing her course work.

Jo Rowling waves from a train in London during the launch of her fourth book, *Harry Potter and the Goblet of Fire.*

Exactly one year after her promise to herself, Jo finished *Harry Potter and the Philosopher's Stone*. She went over the manuscript carefully, rewriting and polishing. Finally, she had the book exactly the way she wanted it. Photocopying the manuscript was too expensive, so Jo used a second-hand typewriter she had managed to buy and typed up two complete copies. She worried about the manuscript's length. The acceptable length for a children's novel was 40,000 words, but her manuscript was more than twice that—90,000 words.

Jo might have had misgivings, but, at long last, she had completed her manuscript. Five years after the idea of a boy wizard popped into her head while she sat on a train, Jo Rowling was ready to see if she could get her first book published.

CHAPTER 6

HARRY POTTER MEETS THE WORLD

Children look at Harry Potter merchandise at a department store in Seoul, South Korea.

Jo was ready to send *Harry Potter and the Philosopher's Stone* to a publisher, but would anyone accept it? She had heard stories about the importance of finding a literary agent if you wanted to be published. At the local library, she found a writer's directory that listed the names and addresses of agents. Nervous but determined, she copied the names of agents she felt might be interested in her work.

Home from the library, Jo slid three chapters of the manuscript into a black plastic folder and mailed it to the first agent on her list. The agent rejected it. She tried sending it to a publisher, but the publisher rejected it. Disappointed but still determined, she again looked at her agent list and came across the name Christopher Little. She liked his name, and she sent him the first three chapters of her manuscript.

Fierce Competition

You've written a book. Now what do you do? Years ago, writers were often successful in sending their manuscripts directly to publishers. Today, most publishing companies prefer to read manuscripts sent to them by an established literary agent who knows the market and can negotiate **contracts** on behalf of a writer. More often than not, however, it can be as difficult to find an agent willing to accept you as it is to find a publisher. In the world of writing and publishing, competition is fierce.

"THE BEST LETTER OF MY LIFE"

Bryony Evens, who worked at the Christopher Little Literary Agency in London, opened Jo Rowling's folder. She took a quick glance at the manuscript and dropped it into the rejection pile. She thought it was a children's book, and their agency did not usually represent authors of children's books. But before she left work that day, Bryony noticed that Jo Rowling's manuscript had hand-drawn illustrations. She lifted the folder out of the rejection pile and took a closer look. Liking what she saw, Bryony suggested to Christopher Little that they ask Joanne Rowling to send the complete manuscript. He agreed.

One day, a letter arrived from the Christopher Little Literary Agency. Jo Rowling tore open the envelope. "I assumed it was a rejection note," she later recalled. "But inside the envelope there was a letter saying 'Thank you. We would be pleased to represent your manuscript on an exclusive basis.' It was the best letter of my life. I read it eight times."

"All I Ever Wanted"

From his experience as a literary agent, Christopher Little knew that authors of children's books made very little money and seldom, if ever, wound up being famous. He warned Jo, "I don't want you going away from this meeting thinking you're going to make a fortune." As Jo later recalled, "Then I said to him, 'I know I'm not going to make any money out of it. I know I'm not going to be famous.' All I ever wanted was for somebody to publish Harry so I could go to bookshops and see it."

A PUBLISHER AT LAST

For a full year, the Christopher Little agency mailed Jo's manuscript to some of the biggest publishers in England. All of them rejected it, and Jo's hopes faded. But Christopher Little encouraged her, saying that the book was too good not to be picked up at some point.

At last, in 1996, *Harry Potter and the Philosopher's Stone* found a home with British publisher Bloomsbury

Harry Potter fans in Malaysia waited in line for hours to buy the much-awaited fifth Harry Potter book, *Harry Potter and the Order of the Phoenix.*

Press. When she heard the news, Jo was beside herself with joy. "It was comparable only to having my daughter," she said.

Jo went to London to meet with the publisher and her agent. One of the details they needed to work out was Jo's pen name. She had signed the manuscript Joanne Rowling. After explaining that young boys might not want to read *Harry Potter and the Philosopher's Stone* if they knew it was written by a woman, the publisher asked Jo if she would mind using her first two initials instead of her first name. But Jo's parents had never given her a middle name. Jo thought of her late, beloved grandmother, Kathleen. She liked the sound of "J" followed by "K," as in the alphabet, and the publisher also liked it. Everyone agreed that Jo's pen name would now be J. K. Rowling.

After the meeting, Jo went to a store. With her first check from the publisher, she bought her daughter Jessica a toy.

OUT OF POVERTY

While production for her first novel was in process, Jo received her teacher's certificate and began looking for a teaching position. She also heard about a Scottish Arts Council grant for authors and applied. Her life was finally looking up. She found a job teaching French, and she also got the grant so she could write *Harry Potter and the Chamber of Secrets*. The grant of $13,000 was the largest sum of money she had ever received at one time. Jo used some of the money to buy a computer to finish her second book. She beamed happily at the ease of deleting a line. Buying the computer had put an end to retyping her longhand manuscripts on her old second-hand typewriter.

On June 26, 1997, Bloomsbury Press published *Harry Potter and the Philosopher's Stone*. When Jo received her copy, she walked all over Edinburgh holding the book under her arm. She peeked in every bookstore window hoping to see it on display. She swears that the first two words her daughter Jessica could read were "Harry" and "Potter."

HARRY GOES INTERNATIONAL

One night, Christopher Little called Jo long distance from New York, where an auction was being held for the international publishing rights to her book. Arthur Levine, the vice president of Scholastic Books in the United States, had just broken all bidding records for an unknown author's first work of fiction for children. Jo nearly fainted. Little also told her that Mr. Levine would be phoning her shortly. Jo's anxiety grew. She was excited and afraid at the same time. She had hoped that the sales from her book would allow her to continue writing, but she had not expected all of this. The telephone rang at eleven p.m. After talking a long time about the book, Mr. Levine said, "Don't be scared." Jo said, "Thanks, I am."

For two hours after her conversation with Levine, Jo walked around her apartment in a "nervous frenzy." After checking in on Jessica, she finally went to bed. "But I couldn't sleep," she later recalled. "On one level, I was obviously delighted, but most of me was just frozen in terror."

Changes for the U.S. Edition

Although English is the official language of both Great Britain and the United States, there are many differences in how the language is spoken and written in the two countries. Jo Rowling's U.S. publisher, Scholastic, wanted her to make some changes for the U.S. edition, including the title, to make the book more appropriate for American readers. Jo came up with the title *Harry Potter and the Sorcerer's Stone*. The publisher also asked Jo to change "mum" to "mom," but she refused. She did change the word "jumper," which refers to a sweater in Great Britain but to a girl's dress in the United States.

Jo Rowling signs copies of *Harry Potter and the Order of the Phoenix* for elementary school children at a bookstore in Edinburgh.

"Quite an Obscure Book"

"I didn't think it [the first Harry Potter book] would do this well with anyone," Jo Rowling has said. "I thought I was writing quite an **obscure** book that, if it ever got published, would maybe have a handful of devotees. ... I never expected it to have broad appeal."

THE SUCCESS OF HARRY POTTER

People everywhere seemed to love Jo's book. In Great Britain, it won a number of important book awards, including the Nestle Smarties Book Prize, the Federation of Children's Books Group Award and the British Book Awards Children's Book of the Year. In 1998, book sales reached a half million—an amount that was unheard of for a children's book.

While her first book became an award-winning best-seller, Jo completed her second book, *Harry Potter and the Chamber of Secrets*. When Bloomsbury published the second book in the summer of 1998, it immediately shot to number one on best-seller lists.

A NEW WAY OF LIFE

The publicity that now surrounded the Harry Potter books terrified Jo Rowling. She has said she was "scared-stiff" by all the attention. She also worried whether the rest of the Harry Potter series would be as popular.

With money she received from book sales, Jo was beginning to adjust to the idea of not being poor. She and Jessica moved to a house in a middle-class neighborhood in Edinburgh. Five-year-old Jessica now had her own room, and Jo was able to write full time. They soon acquired a cat named Chaos, a black rabbit with wild habits that Jessica

named Jemina, a guinea pig they called Jasmine, and a tank of tropical fish.

For Jo, part of the price of publicity was having to travel around the world for book signings and appearances at schools. At one point, she sat in a car that was making its way to a bookstore in Boston, Massachusetts. She asked the driver if there was a good sale going on because people had lined up around the block. When Jo learned that the people were lined up to see her, she was shocked. She tried to look friendly, but all the while she felt terrified. In all, she signed 1,400 books that day.

Jo Rowling found it difficult trying to write the third book, *Harry Potter and the Prisoner of Azkaban*. With all the interviews, book signings, lectures, and school appearances, Jo had less time to write. She loved the idea of meeting with the children who were reading her books, but she had to cut down a little on traveling so she could finish the third book in the series. By now, Jo was beginning to understand what it meant to be famous.

Eager fans await the first copies of *Harry Potter and the Order of the Phoenix.*

A scene from *Harry Potter and the Prisoner of Azkaban.*

POTTERMANIA

Jo Rowling has break-
fast with ten-year-old
Nick Drews, a winner
of an essay contest
sponsored by Scholastic
called "How the Harry
Potter Books Changed
my Life."

Only days after its release in the United States, *Harry Potter and the Prisoner of Azkaban* soared to the top of the *New York Times* best-seller list— followed by the two other Harry Potter books, at spots two and three. "Pottermania" was sweeping the world. By mid-2002, the books in the Harry Potter series had sold 150 million copies worldwide and had been published in fifty languages. Around the world, the Harry Potter books had created a whole new interest in fantasy literature.

MOVIE RIGHTS

In October 1998, Jo and her agent sold the movie rights to the Harry Potter series to Warner Brothers for $2 million. Jo has admitted to being excited and nervous at the prospect of seeing Harry on the big screen. The movie's director, Chris Columbus, flew to Scotland to meet Jo. Both Jo and Columbus came away from the meeting enthusiastic about the film. Columbus said that his ten-year-old daughter had gotten him to read the Harry Potter books. Between his four kids and their friends, he told Jo, he had heard a lot about what the movie should be. "I won't let anyone down," he said.

A Priceless Gift

Just before the publication of the fourth Harry Potter book, *Harry Potter and the Goblet of Fire*, Jo Rowling broke her rule never to let anyone read a book before it was published. Nine-year-old cancer patient Catie Hoch had just finished the third book when her family found out that she had only weeks to live. Catie's mother contacted Jo and told her how much the Harry Potter books meant to her daughter and that Catie would not live long enough to read the fourth book. Jo then called Catie at home almost every day to read to her from *Goblet of Fire* before it was published.

Catie's mother told a reporter, "I will be forever grateful for what Joanne did. She gave us something priceless by having this relationship with Catie."

FAME AND FORTUNE

By the time the fourth Harry Potter book hit bookstores, Jo Rowling had become a celebrity. Journalists and photographers began knocking on her door at all hours. Fan mail was taking over the house. Jo decided to move. She

The Crown Prince of Spain, Felipe de Borbon, presents Jo Rowling with the 2003 Prince of Asturias Award for promoting world harmony through her books. The award is given to someone who has helped "the struggle against injustice, poverty, disease or ignorance, to opening new horizons of knowledge."

bought a larger, more private home in Edinburgh and hired a full-time secretary to help answer the telephone and fan mail. She still loved to write in cafes, but she had to give up her beloved Nicolson's because fans and journalists continuously interrupted her. She did, however, find cafes in out of the way places where she could write in secret, undisturbed.

Following the publication of *Harry Potter and the Goblet of Fire*, Jo Rowling's **alma mater**, the University of Exeter, awarded her an honorary Doctor of Letters degree. Naturally shy, Jo shook with nerves before delivering her acceptance speech. Once on stage, however, she relaxed a bit and gave a talk to which all the graduating students could relate. She started out by reading a postcard from an old friend from Exeter, who wrote to her about the honorary degree : "I assume this is to show the new graduates that you can make something of your life even if you spend three years in The Black Horse [a pub]." From that moment onward, Jo had the graduates in the palm of her hand, and at the end of her speech, she received a rousing ovation.

Groups Against Harry

Critics have praised the Harry Potter books since they first were published, and most teachers have expressed appreciation to J. K. Rowling for helping to create an interest in reading among children. But Harry Potter books have also drawn criticism. At first, some religious groups claimed the books promoted witchcraft, devil worship, and other **occult** activities. Many groups sent letters of protest to newspapers and tried to get the Harry Potter books removed from schools, libraries, and bookstores. A few teachers ordered pupils not to read the Harry Potter tales. Some of the books' detractors cited examples of immorality, such as Harry and his friend Ron cheating on their homework, Ron's mischievous older brothers stealing food from the kitchens, and Harry lying to his friend Hagrid, the giant groundskeeper at Hogwarts. Some even claimed that Harry Potter's lightning bolt scar on his forehead was a mark of the devil.

In Alamogordo, New Mexico, members of the Christ Community Church stand around a bonfire of Harry Potter books and other books that the pastor of the church called satanic.

Not all religious groups were against the books. Some groups said that Rowling's books emphasized the victory of good over evil. Supporters of the Harry Potter books asserted that all children grow up with imaginary worlds full of fairies, magicians, angels, and witches, and that Jo's fantasy tales were not likely to cause a child to practice witchcraft.

Surprised by the controversy, Jo pointed out that Harry and his friends are fighting against evil, not promoting it. "These books are fundamentally moral," she said. Harry and his friends Hermione and Ron all have a strong sense of honor. In the end, Jo chose to ignore opposition to her books, and eventually the storm of protest passed.

Jo Rowling and British comedian Lenny Henry sport red noses for Red Nose Day, a Comic Relief charity event.

Once Jo became wealthy and famous, she began to use both her money and her name to help others. Comic Relief, a charity that raises money for needy and abused people around the world through the use of humor, asked Jo for help. Having experienced poverty as a single mother, she was more than willing to offer her services. As a gift to Comic Relief, Jo wrote two books. *Quidditch Through the Ages* tells all about Quidditch, the game played by Harry Potter and the other students at Hogwarts, and *Fantastic Beasts and Where to Find Them* gives full descriptions of the various kinds of dragons at Hogwarts. All the proceeds from the two books go directly to people in need.

Jo also contributes to the Multiple Sclerosis Society, in honor of her mother. She has advocated for more money for MS research, as well as for pain-relieving drugs and more accessible therapies for MS sufferers. Jo does not want people with MS to go without care—the way her mother often did—because they cannot afford in-home therapy.

In addition, Jo is an ambassador for, and contributor to, the National Council of One Parent Families. This London-based organization helps single mothers with children who are in need. Jo Rowling has never forgotten Prime Minister John Major's speech calling single parents freeloaders. Single parents, Jo has said, are already doing the jobs of two people before they even start looking for paid work. "As I found out the hard way," she says, "we have to fight twice as hard to get half as far."

"Meeting the Queen"

On a visit to her publisher's offices in London, Jo Rowling met the Queen of England. The queen spoke to her about her own love of reading as a child and also mentioned that her grand-daughter was a huge fan of Harry Potter. Later, when Jo received the Order of the British Empire (OBE) award, Prince Charles told her that both he and his son Prince Harry were Harry Potter fans. Prince Charles said, "I'm staggered that someone can write so beautifully."

Jo Rowling with British queen Elizabeth II

A NEW FAMILY

Despite the demands of her fame, Jo wanted to have more children—but first she had to find the right person with which to have them. One day, she was introduced to a physician, Dr. Neil Murray, who very much resembles a grown-up version of Harry Potter. It was love at first sight, and Jessica liked Neil, too. Following a steady courtship, Jo and Neil were married on December 27, 2001. They had a small wedding with family and friends, away from journalists and photographers, and the wedding guests were sworn to secrecy.

Jo Rowling with her husband Neil Murray

After the wedding, the couple didn't go on a honeymoon. Instead, Jo worked on her fifth book, *Harry Potter and the Order of the Phoenix*, eagerly awaited by millions of children throughout the world.

In March 2003, just three months before *Harry Potter and the Order of the Phoenix* went on sale, Jo Rowling gave birth to a baby boy, whom she named David. Her life had come a long way from her first years in Edinburgh. She had achieved fantastic success as a writer, she was married to a man she adored, and her beloved daughter now had a baby brother.

A BOY NAMED HARRY

Harry Potter, meanwhile, continues to attract fans worldwide. The fourth Harry Potter book, *Harry Potter and the Goblet of Fire*, is the fastest selling book in history—three million copies were sold in the first forty-eight hours of its release. Book five, *Harry Potter and the Order of the Phoenix*, broke records when nearly nine million copies were printed, an unprecedented amount for any book. With over 170 million copies sold, the Harry Potter books have been translated into fifty-five languages and distributed in countries around the world. The five books are also currently on the best-seller lists around the world. Warner Brothers, which plans to make each Harry Potter book into a movie, released the movie version of *Harry Potter and the Chamber of Secrets* in 2002. The movie version of *Harry Potter and the Prisoner of Azkaban* was released in 2004.

Like Harry Potter, Jo Rowling has become a celebrity, and her life has changed dramatically since her days as a struggling single mother. But one thing has not changed. Jo Rowling still loves to write about the adventures of a special boy named Harry Potter, and she still uses the power of her imagination to create a unique, magical world.

TIMELINE

1965	Joanne Rowling is born on July 31 in Chipping Sodbury, England
1971	Writes first story. Family moves to Winterbourne
1974	Moves to Tutshill. Writes *The Seven Cursed Diamonds*
1976	Enters Wyedean Comprehensive School in Chepstow
1979	Mother diagnosed with multiple sclerosis
1983	Enrolls at the University of Exeter
1987	Graduates from Exeter with a degree in French
1990	Begins work on *Harry Potter and the Philosopher's Stone.* Mother dies at age forty-five of multiple sclerosis
1991	Moves to Oporto, Portugal, to teach English
1992	Marries Jorge Arantes
1993	Gives birth to daughter, Jessica. Leaves Jorge and moves to Edinburgh, Scotland, with daughter
1994	Accepts welfare while finishing *Harry Potter and the Philosopher's Stone*
1995	Finishes *Harry Potter and the Philosopher's Stone*
1997	Receives a $13,000 grant from Scottish Arts Council. *Harry Potter and the Philosopher's Stone* (U.S. title, *Harry Potter and the Sorcerer's Stone*) is published. Wins Nestle Smarties prize
1998	*Harry Potter and the Chamber of Secrets* is published. Rowling sells movie rights to Warner Brothers.
1999	*Harry Potter and the Prisoner of Azkaban* is published
2000	*Harry Potter and the Goblet of Fire* is published
2001	The movie *Harry Potter and the Sorcerer's Stone* hits theaters. Rowling marries Dr. Neil Murray
2002	The movie *Harry Potter and the Chamber of Secrets* is released
2003	Rowling gives birth to son, David. *Harry Potter and the Order of the Phoenix* is published
2004	The movie *Harry Potter and the Prisoner of Azkaban* is released; the title of the sixth book in the series, *Harry Potter and the Half Blood Prince*, is announced; the movie version of *Harry Potter and the Goblet of Fire* is announced

activist: a person who seeks change through protests, demonstrations, and other means.

alma mater: the college, university, or other school from which a person has graduated.

bilingual: having to do with two languages.

civil rights: the basic rights belonging to every citizen of a country.

contracts: agreements that are enforceable by law and often establish business arrangements, such as between a publisher and a writer.

counselor: a person who offers advice to people, usually in order to help them with their problems.

feminist: a person who seeks rights and opportunities for women equal to those of men.

flat: in Great Britain, an apartment that occupies just one floor of a building.

literary agent: a person who helps writers find publishers for their work and represents the writers in business matters, such as contracts with publishers.

manuscript: the text of a book that has not yet been set in type by a publisher.

muckraker: a writer who exposes wrongdoing by companies or people.

mythology: a body of myths, which are stories told by a certain group of people to explain their beliefs, practices, and experiences with the natural world. Myths often include heroes and gods.

netball: a game that is similar to basketball, in which two teams of seven players each score goals by throwing a ball through a hoop and net at the top of a pole.

obscure: not known by very many people.

occult: having to do with supernatural or magical activities, forces, or beings.

pen name: the name that an author uses for a published work.

social worker: a person whose job is to help poor or troubled people.

welfare: a program in which the government provides money or other forms of aid to people in need. In Great Britain, welfare is known as public assistance.

TO FIND OUT MORE

BOOKS

Beahm, George W. *Muggles and Magic: J. K. Rowling and the Harry Potter Phenomenon*. Charlottesville, Va.: Hampton Roads Publishing, 2004.

Chippendale, Lisa A. *Triumph of the Imagination: The Story of Writer J. K. Rowling (Overcoming Adversity)*. Philadelphia: Chelsea House Publishers, 2002.

Compson, William. *J. K. Rowling (Library of Author Biographies*. New York: Rosen Publishing, 2003.

Fraser, Lindsey. *Conversations with J. K. Rowling*. New York: Scholastic, 2001.

Gaines, Ann. *J. K. Rowling: A Real-Life Reader Biography*. Bear, Del.: Mitchell Lane Publishers, 2002.

McCarthy, Shaun. *J. K. Rowling (All About)*. Chicago: Raintree, 2004.

INTERNET SITES

Bloomsbury Publishing
www.bloomsbury.com/harrypotter
This web site from the British publisher of Harry Potter has a message board, news, and the Bloomsbury Web Club.

Harry Potter and the Prisoner of Azkaban
www.harrypotter.warnerbros.com/
A web site from Warner Brothers that includes a message board and games.

J. K. Rowling Official Site
www.jkrowling.com
The official web site from J. K. Rowling, which includes a biography.

Scholastic Publishing
http://www.scholastic.com/harrypotter/home.asp
The web site from the U.S. publisher of Harry Potter includes discussion groups and a pronunciation guide.

Stories from the Web
www.storiesfromtheweb.org/Stories/rowling/interview1.asp
Read an interview with J. K. Rowling.

INDEX *(continued)*

About the Author

Joan Price has a Ph.D. from Arizona State University. She is professor emeritus of philosophy at Mesa Community College. In 2003, she was named one of the 2000 most important scholars of the twentieth century. Joan has written dozens of books and papers and is the author of *Truth Is a Bright Star*, a Native-American tale for children. She is an animal lover with two Weimaraner dogs, two alley cats, and several flocks of wild geese and ducks that camp on the lake by her house for daily handouts. She lives in Scottsdale, Arizona.